Stopwatch Puzzles

Stopwatch Puzzles

Helene Hovanec

Sterling Publishing Co., Inc.
New York

**Library of Congress Cataloging-in-Publication
Data Available**

2   4   6   8   10   9   7   5   3

Published in 2004 by Sterling Publishing Co., Inc.
387 Park Avenue South, New York, NY 10016
Copyright © 2004 by Helene Hovanec
Memory Tests Copyright © 2004 by Fraser Simpson
Illustration on pages 12 and 13 Copyright © 2004
by John Ueland
Distributed in Canada by Sterling Publishing
c/o Canadian Manda Group
165 Dufferin Street,
Toronto, Ontario, Canada M6K 3H6
Distributed in Great Britain and Europe by
Chris Lloyd at Orca Book Services, Stanley House,
Fleets Lane, Poole BH15 3AJ, England
Distributed in Australia by
Capricorn Link (Australia) Pty Ltd.
P.O. Box 704, Windsor, NSW 2756, Australia

Manufactured in China
All Rights Reserved

Sterling ISBN 1-4027-0580-8

Introduction

It's about time! Finally, a kids' puzzle book that records your solving times on puzzles.

Maybe you're a speed demon, or a methodic, slow solver, or perhaps you are somewhere in between. It doesn't matter; you probably just want to know how your solving time compares to that of kids in your age group.

Set the minutes on your stopwatch according to the "suggested time" limit of each puzzle. There's also room for you to record your actual solving time. You may be super speedy at some puzzles and much slower at others. Don't worry; just record your solving times. When you're finished with the book, you'll have a written record of how long you needed to solve each puzzle.

Here are a few hints for you:

* Always read the directions so you know what you actually have to do.
* Start with any letters already in a grid so that you can start filling it in quickly.
* In a hidden answer word search be sure to circle each listed word very carefully so that you'll be able to find the LEFTOVER letters quickly.
* There's no right or wrong way to solve a puzzle. You can start anywhere and go through the puzzle in any order you like.
* Don't take time to laugh at the corny jokes—you can do that when you've finished the puzzle.
* Finally, and most importantly, have fun!

Food Fun

Find and circle the 19 foods on this list in the grid on the opposite page. Look up, down, and diagonally both forward and backward. When all the words have been circled take the LEFTOVER letters and write them in the blanks below the grid. Go from left to right and top to bottom to finish this riddle: Why did the silly kids attach rockets to their hamburgers? Because they . . .

BACON

BREAD

CREAM PUFF

EGGS

FRUIT

HASH

LIVER

ONION

PEAS

PORK

POT PIE

PUDDING

RICE

SALAD

SALAMI

SAUSAGE

SOUP

TUNA

VEAL

```
S  L  I  S  A  L  A  D  P
A  N  O  I  N  O  A  O  U
E  U  L  I  V  E  R  T  D
P  S  S  E  R  K  K  U  D
O  E  A  B  A  C  O  N  I
T  L  U  L  T  D  F  A  N
P  A  S  S  A  I  T  F  G
I  H  A  S  H  M  U  O  O
E  G  G  S  E  C  I  R  D
C  R  E  A  M  P  U  F  F
```

Riddle Answer: __ __ __ __ __ __   __ __ __ __ __ __ __ __ .

Suggested Time: 20

Your Time: _____

Answer on page 87

ALPHA-RIDDLE

Put the words on this page into the grid on the opposite page in ALPHABETICAL ORDER. Then read down one of the columns to find the two-word answer to this riddle: What do you call four stone Presidents with a skin condition?

ANGERED

AMERICAN

AIMLESS

AFRAID

ADEPT

ACCOUNT

ACCORD

ABDOMEN

ADDING

ADORABLE

AGHAST

AHOY

ALLOWANCE

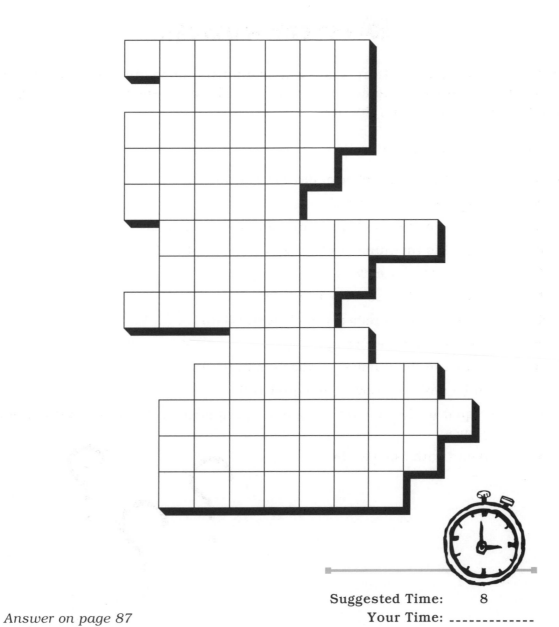

Answer on page 87

Suggested Time: 8

Your Time: -------------

Mystery number

One dozen numbers that are scattered around the opposite page are described below. Cross off each one as you identify it. The one remaining is the mystery number. How fast can you find it?

Eliminate the number that . . .

A . . . is equal to the number of days in two weeks

B . . . rhymes with "dirty door"

C . . . is equal to the number of minutes in ½ hour plus 6

D . . . is equal to the number of weeks in a year plus 2

E . . . rhymes with "late clean"

F . . . is equal to 25 + 25 + 25 + 25 - 25

G . . . is equal to the number of nickels in $3.35

H . . . is equal to 3 times 21

 I . . . is equal to the number of quarters in $4.25

J . . . can be multiplied by 11 to equal 165

K . . . is equal to the amount of money in 2 quarters, 2 dimes, 1 nickel, and 4 pennies

L . . . rhymes with "sporty shoe"

Suggested Time: 5
Your Time: -------------

Answer on page 87

11

Memory Test 1: At the Bus Platform

How good is your memory? Study this scene for up to three (3) minutes, and then turn the page and answer the questions. Once you turn the page, you are relying solely on your memory of what you've seen.

Memory Test 1 Questions

Stop! Don't read these questions until you have looked at the picture on the previous page.

1. A woman is entering a bus. What is she carrying?
2. Where is the bus headed?
3. How many scoops are on the young girl's ice cream cone?
4. A man looks at his watch: how many pockets does his overcoat have?
5. How many suitcases does the family have with them?
6. How many dogs (the animals, not the food item) appear in the picture?
7. How much does a hot dog and a drink cost?
8. At what time does the next bus leave?
9. Does the vendor's shirt have horizontal or vertical stripes?
10. Is the child holding the balloon wearing a dress or shorts?

Answer on page 87

END/START

Take a word from the box and write it on each line to form the end of a six-letter word and the start of a seven-letter word. Cross off each word as you use it.

ALL	ANT	BAT	BED	CAT
COT	EAR	ESS	FIN	LOT
MAT	PET	ROT	ROW	TIC

1. M A S __ __ __ T A G E

2. P A R __ __ __ U N D A

3. B O B __ __ __ A L O G

4. C O M __ __ __ H T U B

5. T A C __ __ __ K L E D

6. M U F __ __ __ A L L Y

7. O C E __ __ __ T E R Y

8. C A R __ __ __ U N I A

9. R U B __ __ __ R O O M

10. F O R __ __ __ A D O R

11. M U T __ __ __ O N Y M

12. S O R __ __ __ B O A T

13. R E C __ __ __ E R G Y

14. A P P __ __ __ A C H E

15. U N L __ __ __ E N C E

Suggested Time: 6

Your Time: _____

Answer on page 87

15

ANSWERING SERVICE

Figure out the answers to the four clues and write each letter on a numbered blank. Then transfer the letters to the same numbered blanks below to answer this riddle:

Where can you always find diamonds?

Like 5 or 7

$$\frac{}{8} \quad \frac{}{4} \quad \frac{}{13}$$

Front part of the head

$$\frac{}{9} \quad \frac{}{3} \quad \frac{}{6} \quad \frac{}{5}$$

Ill

$$\frac{}{14} \quad \frac{}{1} \quad \frac{}{10} \quad \frac{}{7}$$

Took part in a marathon

$$\frac{}{12} \quad \frac{}{11} \quad \frac{}{2}$$

Answer:

$$\frac{}{1} \quad \frac{}{2} \quad \frac{}{3} \quad \frac{}{4} \quad \frac{}{5} \quad \frac{}{6} \quad \frac{}{7} \quad \frac{}{8} \quad \frac{}{9} \quad \frac{}{10} \quad \frac{}{11} \quad \frac{}{12} \quad \frac{}{13} \quad \frac{}{14}$$

Now repeat what you did on the opposite page to answer this riddle: What do ghosts put in their cereal?

Adore

$\overline{}_{13}$ $\overline{}_{5}$ $\overline{}_{2}$ $\overline{}_{9}$

Angry

$\overline{}_{11}$ $\overline{}_{7}$ $\overline{}_{10}$

Grassy area with a playground

$\overline{}_{4}$ $\overline{}_{3}$ $\overline{}_{6}$ $\overline{}_{14}$

Man's neckwear

$\overline{}_{8}$ $\overline{}_{12}$ $\overline{}_{1}$

Answer:

$\overline{}_{1}$ $\overline{}_{2}$ $\overline{}_{3}$ $\overline{}_{4}$ $\overline{}_{5}$ $\overline{}_{6}$ $\overline{}_{7}$ $\overline{}_{8}$ $\overline{}_{9}$ $\overline{}_{10}$ $\overline{}_{11}$ $\overline{}_{12}$ $\overline{}_{13}$ $\overline{}_{14}$

Answer on page 87

Suggested Time: 8
Your Time: _____

NOT SO SYMBOL

How quickly can you find the 6 squares which are exactly like the one in the top right corner? Circle each one as you find it.

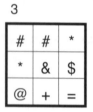

#	#	*
*	&	$
@	+	=

1

*	#	*
*	&	$
@	+	=

2

#	#	*
*	&	$
@	+	=

3

#	#	*
*	&	$
@	+	=

4

*	#	#
=	$	&
@	=	=

5

#	#	*
&	&	$
@	+	=

6

#	#	*
*	&	$
+	@	=

7

#	#	*
*	*	&
@	+	=

8

#	#	*
*	&	$
@	+	=

9

#	#	*
*	&	$
@	=	+

10

#	#	*
*	&	$
@	+	=

11

*	#	*
*	$	&
@	+	=

12

#	#	@
*	&	$
*	+	=

13

*	#	#
=	$	&
@	=	=

14

#	#	*
*	&	$
@	+	=

15

*	#	*
=	$	&
@	+	=

16

#	#	*
&	&	$
@	+	=

17

#	#	*
*	*	&
@	+	=

18

#	#	*
*	&	$
@	+	=

Suggested Time: 3
Your Time: _____

Answer on page 88

HAPPY/SAD

Unscramble 8 synonyms for LAUGH and write them on the lines. Spelling counts!

GLEGIG   _____

WOHL   _____

KARCC PU   _____

HULKECC   _____

MILES   _____

INGR   _____

ORRA   _____

STURB A UGT   _____

Now do the same thing with 8 synonyms for CRY.

OBS   _____

EWEP   _____

ALIW   _____

KABRE OWND   _____

LUBERBB   _____

BLAW   _____

HIPMWRE   _____

KRIESH   _____

Answer on page 88

Suggested Time: 3

Your Time: ------------

◎N THE ROAD

Each word contains a different number of letters, from 4 to 11. Place each word into the only space it will fit into. Then read down one of the columns to find another word for TRAFFIC JAM.

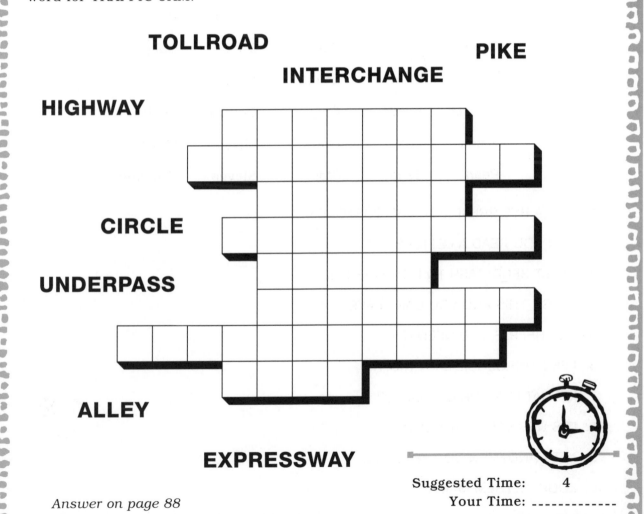

TOLLROAD

INTERCHANGE

PIKE

HIGHWAY

CIRCLE

UNDERPASS

ALLEY

EXPRESSWAY

Suggested Time: 4

Your Time: _____

Answer on page 88

HIDDEN NAMES

The names in the box below are hidden between two or more words in these silly sentences. Underline each one as you find it.

Adam	Andrew	Arnold	Ashton	Bill
Carol	Chris	Dale	Doris	Doug
Eartha	Ellen	Emma	Ethan	Ethel
Frances	Frieda	Gary	George	Ingrid
Jason	Leon	Linda	Mary	Mona
Pearl	Sandy	Stan	Steven	Theodore

1. BAG A RYE BREAD FOR THE CUSTOMER.

2. CAN YOU READ A LETTER?

3. DON'T SEND CASH TO NEW FRIENDS.

4. FINISH THIS AND YOU CAN LEAVE.

5. GET HELP IF YOU NEED IT.

6. I FED THE GERBIL LAST NIGHT.

7. IS THAT LEAD OR IS IT GOLD?

8. IT'S HER EAR THAT HURTS.

9. LET HANDYMEN DO THE WORK.

10. LOOK AT THEM MAMA!

11. SHE CAN'T SELL ENOUGH CLOTHING.

12. SHE LOST A NEW COAT.

13. SHE'S LEARNING RIDICULOUS JOKES.

14. THAT COMPANY WILL MERGE OR GET SOLD.

15. THE COOK FRIED APPLES.

16. THE WOMAN DREW PORTRAITS.

17. WALK A MILE ON SUNDAY.

18. WE WENT OUT LAST EVENING.

19. WHICH RISK WILL HE TAKE?

20. YOU SHOULD VISIT FRANCE SOON.

21. IS THE BARN OLDER THAN THE HOUSE?

22. DON'T MAR YOUR COUNTER TOP.

23. I HAD A MEAL AT THE DINER.

24. THE MARLIN DARTED ABOUT.

25. THE ODOR EMANATED FROM THE KITCHEN.

26. THREE RAJAS ONLY WANTED TO SING.

27. DO UGLY PETS GET PAMPERED?

28. IS YOUR CAR OLDER THAN MINE?

29. I AM ON A DIET.

30. HAVE YOU HAD A PEAR LATELY?

Answer on page 88

Suggested Time: 12
Your Time: --------------

MAKEOVERS

Each seven-letter word on this page had its letters rearranged into a two-word phrase on the opposite page. Match up each word with its made-over phrase by placing the letter of the phrase in the blank on each line.

1. CANTEEN _____
2. COMPARE _____
3. COMPETE _____
4. CONSENT _____
5. DISPUTE _____
6. DISTANT _____
7. STAMMER _____
8. EMBARGO _____
9. FLATTER _____
10. FORGERY _____
11. GLAMOUR _____

12. IMPEACH _____
13. LATERAL _____
14. MARRIED _____
15. SLENDER _____
16. NOURISH _____
17. NOVELTY _____
18. OPTICAL _____
19. PIGTAIL _____
20. PROMOTE _____
21. RADIATE _____
22. SHINGLE _____

a. VET ONLY

b. COPE MET

c. TEPID US

d. TEAR ALL

e. SAD TINT

f. RYE FROG

g. RED LENS

h. DARE RIM

i. ACNE NET

j. RACE MOP

k. POEM ROT

l. AMBER GO

m. PAIL COT

n. ACME HIP

o. NO CENTS

p. MET MARS

q. LOAM RUG

r. LEFT ART

s. IN HOURS

t. HIS GLEN

u. ARID EAT

v. GAIT LIP

Answer on page 89

THE WRITE STUFF

If PATTY TURNER is the "author" of HAMBURGER RECIPES, which "writer" on the opposite page is the author of the books listed here? Put the correct name on each line to make your own best-seller list!

1. DANGEROUS STREET CROSSINGS _____

2. CARD GAMES _____

3. DINING OUT ALL THE TIME _____

4. THE DESSERT COOKBOOK _____

5. SYNTHETIC FABRICS _____

6. GAMES FOR TODDLERS _____

7. ROUND ABOUT _____

8. HOW TO MAKE MILLIONS _____

9. CREATIVE JEWELRY _____

10. YEWS, PINES, AND CEDARS _____

11. CALL ME ROMEO _____

12. MIRACLE MEDICINE _____

13. THE BIG CHEESE _____

14. THE MOVING MANUAL _____

VAN DRIVER

ANN T. BIOTIC

HY DAN SEEK

VAL V. TA

STERLING SILVER

RICH MANN

B. SWEET

KENT COOK

HART BRAKER

FOREST RANGER

JAY WALKER

POLLY ESTER

SIR CULL

ACE S. WILDE

Answer on page 89

Suggested Time: 8
Your Time: -------------

STATE DEPARTMENT

Answer the 13 clues by combining two letter groups from the box. Write the answers in the grid on the opposite page, going DOWN. When the grid is filled in, read ACROSS two of the rows to find the names of two states.

ASY	EAD	ESS	EST	GHT
GRE	GUE	HON	INC	INV
ISH	ITE	MAL	MIN	NET
NOR	OME	PLA	PRA	RCH
SCO	STR	TAU	THR	UTE
		VAN		

1. Yearly salary

2. Regular

3. Oily, like fried food

4. Extreme pressure

5. It's on a spool

6. Burn

7. Was a professor

8. Capital of the Czech Republic

9. Word used to describe Abraham Lincoln

10. Mercury or Pluto

11. $\frac{1}{60}$th of an hour

12. Ask to a party

13. Disappear

1	2	3	4	5	6	7	8	9	10	11	12	13

Suggested Time: 15

Your Time: -------------

Answer on page 89

JUST THE OPPOSITE

Change the letter in boldface in each word to another letter and you'll find a pair of opposites on each line. Write the new words on the blanks.

1. WI**G** _____   LO**B**E _____

2. SHAR**K** _____   BLU**R**T _____

3. SMI**T**E _____   **B**ROWN _____

4. **P**EAL _____   **B**AKE _____

5. **L**ICE _____   **D**EAN _____

6. **N**OT _____   **B**OLD _____

7. F**I**ST _____   **B**LOW _____

8. **L**IVE _____   **R**AKE _____

9. **N**AME _____   WIL**L** _____

10. WH**A**LE _____   P**E**RT _____

11. POLI**C**E _____   **D**UDE _____

12. U**S** _____   **M**OWN _____

13. F**I**LL _____   SPRIN**T** _____

Now do the same thing WITHOUT any hints!

14. D O V E _____   D A T E _____

15. D I N E _____   H O U R S _____

16. F A L L _____   S H I R T _____

17. T I D E _____   M A R R O W _____

18 P I C K _____   B E L L _____

19. S A T _____   S H I N _____

20. R I C E _____   M O O R _____

21. B O W _____   S I G H _____

22. O V E N _____   C L O V E _____

23. H O O D _____   F A D _____

24. T A R _____   P E A C H _____

25. S H E E T _____   D O U R _____

26. L I G H T _____   W R I N G _____

Suggested Time: 7

Your Time: _____

Answer on page 89

"P" IS FOR PUZZLE

Each word in this list contains the letter "P." Use the letters that are already in the grid and place every word in its PROPER place.

4 Letters

HARP

PASS

PIER

TAPE

5 Letters

BLIMP

EXPEL

PAPER

PLAID

SCOOP

SPINE

6 Letters

BEEPER

PROPER

RIPPLE

SPIRAL

TYPIST

7 Letters

OPERATE

PLANTER

POMPOUS

PORTION

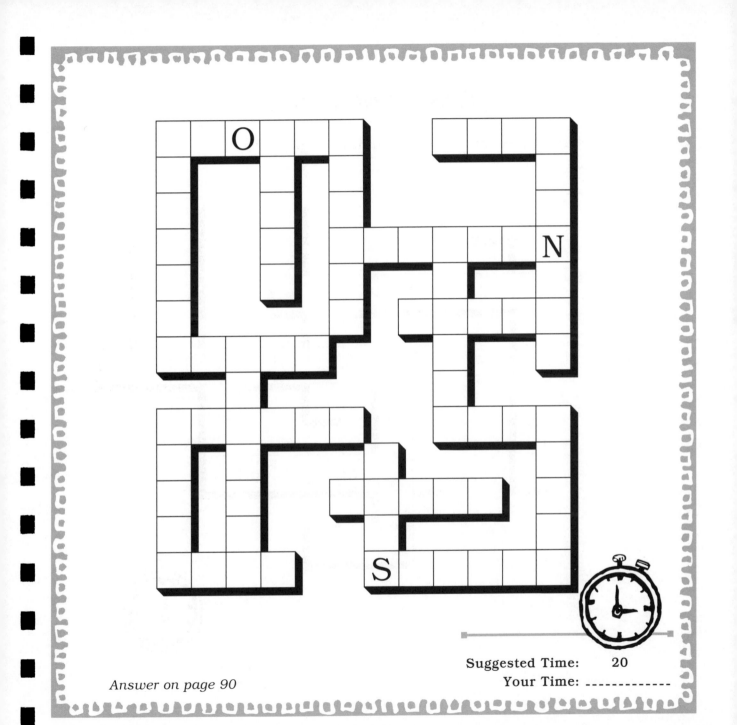

Answer on page 90

Suggested Time: 20
Your Time: ------------

33

CARRYING CASES

Put each carrying case into the grid as quickly as possible!

BACKPACK

BAG

CARRYALL

KIT

LUGGAGE

SATCHEL

SUITCASE

TOTE

TRUNK

VALISE

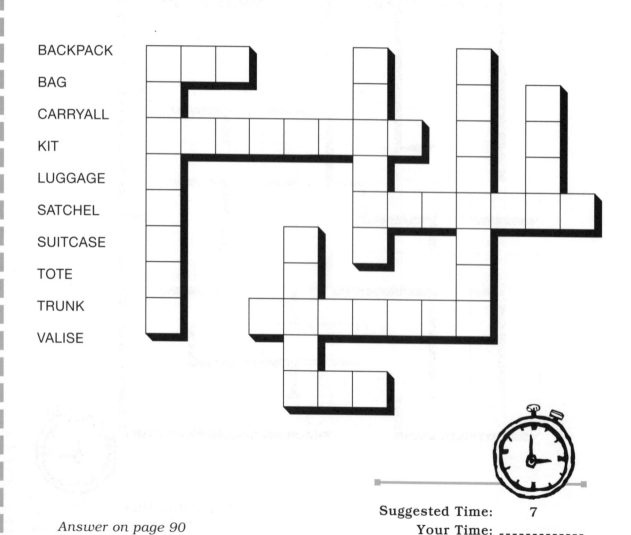

Suggested Time: 7
Your Time: ------------

Answer on page 90

VACATION PLACES

Now put each vacation place into this grid.

BUNGALOW

CABIN

COTTAGE

HOSTEL

HOTEL

LODGE

MOTOR INN

RANCH

RESORT

SPA

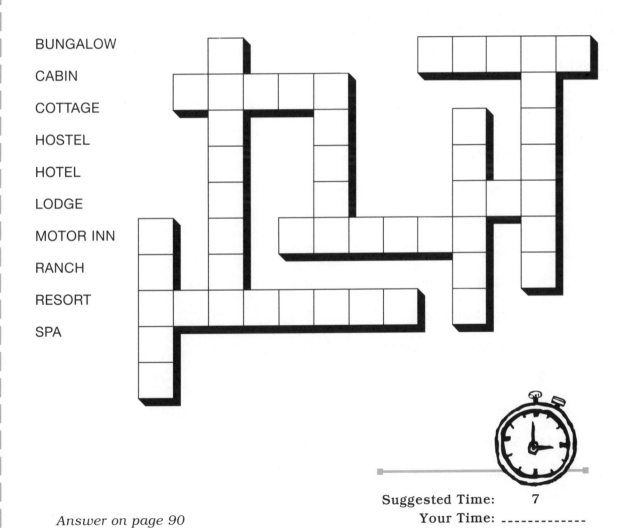

Suggested Time: 7

Your Time: --------------

Answer on page 90

TUNED IN

Read each description and write a two-word rhyming phrase on each line. The number of blank spaces tells you how many letters there are in each word. The first letter of each word has been given to you.

Example: Colorful sleeping spot = RED BED.

Most of the rhymes will be VERY CORNY! Don't let that stop you from working quickly!

1. Finest exam   B _ _ _   T _ _ _

2. Tiny entranceway   S _ _ _ _   H _ _ _

3. Distant auto   F _ _   C _ _

4. Feeble bird's bill   W _ _ _   B _ _ _

5. Phony dessert   F _ _ _   C _ _ _

6. True lunch or dinner R _ _ _   M _ _ _

7. Large hairpiece   B _ _   W _ _

8. Pleasant frozen water N _ _ _   I _ _

9. Jam stomach   J _ _ _ _   B _ _ _ _

10. Evening view   N _ _ _ _   S _ _ _ _

11. Silent hobo   M _ _   B _ _

12. Entire fishing rod   W _ _ _ _   P _ _ _

13.	Prison cry	J _ _ _	W _ _ _
14.	Pastel-colored basin	P _ _ _	S _ _ _
15.	Sixth month eating utensil	J _ _ _	S _ _ _ _
16.	Green coin	L _ _ _	D _ _ _
17.	Obtain plane	G _ _	J _ _
18.	Visitor to a bird's home	N _ _ _	G _ _ _ _
19.	Chilled swimming spot	C _ _ _	P _ _ _
20.	Unused paste	N _ _	G _ _ _
21.	Simple necklace	P _ _ _ _	C _ _ _ _
22.	Bucket's weighing device	P _ _ _	S _ _ _ _
23.	Crate for a sly animal	F _ _	B _ _
24.	Throw finger jewelry	F _ _ _ _	R _ _ _

Suggested Time: 4
Your Time: _____

Answer on page 90

Memory Test 2: The "C" Challenge

How good is your memory? Study this group of 25 objects that begin with the letter "C" for up to three (3) minutes and then close the book. Then list as many items as you can on a piece of paper. You are relying solely on your memory of what you've seen. To help you with scoring, an alphabetical list appears in the answer section.

Answer on page 90

FIRST LADIES

Find the first names of 14 First Ladies by looking up, down, forward, backward, and diagonally. After you've circled those 14 names, put the LEFTOVER letters on the blank lines. Those letters will spell the first and last names of another First Lady.

BARBARA (Bush)

BESS (Truman)

BETTY (Ford)

DOLLEY (Madison)

ELEANOR (Roosevelt)

HELEN (Taft)

HILLARY (Clinton)

JULIA (Grant)

LADY BIRD (Johnson)

LUCY (Hayes)

MAMIE (Eisenhower)

MARTHA (Washington)

NANCY (Reagan)

PAT (Nixon)

N	E	L	E	H	A	J	Y	A
A	E	A	C	I	Q	C	H	U
N	E	L	L	L	U	T	B	Y
C	L	U	E	L	R	I	A	E
Y	J	N	E	A	K	E	R	L
T	N	N	M	R	N	E	B	L
T	A	P	D	Y	Y	O	A	O
E	L	A	D	Y	B	I	R	D
B	E	S	S	E	I	M	A	M

Answer: __ __ __ __ __ __ __ __ __   __ __ __ __ __ __

Suggested Time: 8

Your Time: -------------

Answer on page 90

Squeeze play

Two related words are hidden on each line. The letters of both words are in order, but the words have been tangled together. Use the clues in the [ ] to help you untangle the words. Write them on the blanks.

1. C J O A M R D B O A N D I A
   [Foreign countries]
   _____and_____

2. D I B O T A P E T L E S R S
   [Baby stuff]
   _____and_____

3. C H C A R Y D I L S L E L A C R
   [American cars]
   _____and_____

4. N T O V U E S E M B D E R A Y
   [Calendar words]
   _____and_____

5. C C H O I P U M G U A N R K
   [Animals]
   _____and_____

6. L O C L B S T E A M R S
   [Seafood]
   _____and_____

7. K M E O L S L Y S
   [Shades of green]
   _____and_____

8. N P E U C T A N C R H
   [Drinks]
   _____and_____

9. Y C R O G E U R A M T
   [Dairy products]
   _____and_____

10. H P R A R V I N A C E R T O D N
    [Ivy League schools]
    _____and_____

11. C R B A O D M Q U I N T E T O N
    [Outdoor games]
    _____and_____

12. S C G E O R M I N P I O I
    [Zodiac signs]
    _____and_____

13. P I T H N K I U M E B
[Finger parts]

_____and_____

14. L W I M A L B T Z O
[Dances]

_____and_____

15. O P A M E N C L E A K T E
[Breakfast foods]

_____and_____

16. H U S W N G A E D I R I A S H N
[Languages]

_____and_____

17. S O J P H O U N M O I O R R E
[High-school students]

_____and_____

18. Z B U I P T T P E O N R
[Fasteners]

_____and_____

19. V S O A L A V B O
[Foreign cars]

_____and_____

20. M P R E A Y S I O R D E N T
[Elected Officials]

_____and_____

21. M A R Y A I N N K E R S E E S
[Baseball teams]

_____and_____

22. K J U A R A D T E O
[Martial arts]

_____and_____

23. G E O A L M E T G E B R Y R A
[Math classes]

_____and_____

24. Z E G U G P C C L A H I N T N I
[Vegetables]

_____and_____

Answer on page 91

Suggested Time: 15
Your Time: - - - - - - - - - - - - -

CUT IT OUT

The riddle editor cut out some words (and names) from a joke and placed them in the box below. Can you reconstruct the joke by taking each term below and placing it into the correct spot on the opposite page? Cross off each item as you use it. Don't waste precious time laughing!

AD	AN	AS	ASK	CAUSE	DASH
DO	ELL	EVER	FRO	GAIN	GO
HE	HERE	HIS	IN	JOG	LATE
LICE	LIED	LIT	LOCK	MAN	ME
MOTH	OFF	RED	ROSS	ROUND	RUN
SELF	SHED	TIM	TOP	WAY	WON

A _ _ _ T L E   B O Y   R U _ _ _ _   B Y

A   P O _ _ _ _   _ _ _ I C E R.   F I V E

M _ _ U T E S   _ _ _ R   H E   _ _ _ _ E D

B Y   A _ _ _ _.   A F T E R   _ _ I N G   T _ _ _

S _ _ _ _ A L   T I M E S   T _ _   C O P

S _ _ _ P E D   T H E   B O Y   _ _ D   _ _ _ E D,

" W _ _ _ _   A R E   Y O U   _ _ I N G?"

T H E   K I D   R E P _ _ _ _ _,"I'M   _ _ _ N I G

A _ _ _   _ _ _ M   H O _ _."

" W _ _ _,   W H Y   A R E   Y O U   _ _ _ G I N G

A _ _ _ _ _   T H E   B _ _ _ _   S O   _ _ _ Y

_ _ _ E S?"   _ _ K E D   T H E   C O P.

T H E   K I D   A N S W E _ _ _,   "B E _ _ _ _ _ _

M Y   _ _ _ _ E R   _ _ _'T   L E T   M E

C _ _ _ _   T H E   R O _ _   B Y   M Y _ _ _ _."

Suggested Time: 15
Your Time: ------------

Answer on page 91

Animal Antics

Find the 18 listed animals in the grid on the opposite page. Look up, down, and diagonally both backward and forward. Circle each one as you locate it. After all the words are circled, write the UNUSED letters in the blanks below the grid. Go from left to right and top to bottom and you'll finish this riddle:

How do baby sheep stay cool in the summer? They use . . .

AARDVARK

ALPACA

ANTELOPE

BEAR

BOAR

BOBCAT

BUFFALO

CAMEL

ELK

JACKAL

JAGUAR

KANGAROO

KOALA

LEOPARD

PORCUPINE

RACCOON

RAT

TIGER

```
A  N  T  E  L  O  P  E  A  J
A  L  E  O  P  A  R  D  A  A
R  L  P  L  E  M  A  C  B  G
D  A  B  A  A  M  K  R  U  U
V  R  E  L  C  A  L  A  F  A
A  B  A  S  L  A  E  C  F  R
R  O  R  T  H  A  D  C  A  E
K  A  N  G  A  R  O  O  L  G
E  T  A  C  B  O  B  O  O  I
P  O  R  C  U  P  I  N  E  T
```

Riddle Answer: __   __ __ __ __   __ __ __ __ __

Suggested Time: 20
Your Time: --------------

Answer on page 91

Adventure Travel

You won't find any of the places listed here on a map. That's because there's one mistake on each line. It could be one extra letter, a letter missing, or a word misspelled. Write the real names on the lines.

1. SINGAPOUR   _____

2. NEWT HAMPSHIRE   _____

3. PARISH, FRANCE   _____

4. ROMEO, ITALY   _____

5. SETTLE, WASHINGTON   _____

6. STAN JOSE, CALIFORNIA   _____

7. GRATE LAKES   _____

8. BARTON ROUGE, LOUISIANA   _____

9. KOALA LUMPUR, MALAYSIA   _____

10. ANNAPOLIS, MARRYLAND   _____

11. AMAZON DRIVER   _____

12. RIOT GRANDE   _____

13. POLO ALTO, CALIFORNIA   _____

14. JUSTIN, TEXAS   _____

15. KODAK, ALASKA _____

16. ANN HARBOR, MICHIGAN _____

17. FORT FLEE, NEW JERSEY _____

18. CO-STAR RICA _____

19. EERIE, PENNSYLVANIA _____

20. DREADING, PENNSYLVANIA _____

21. SOUL, KOREA _____

22. WASHINGTON, C.D. _____

23. BURN, SWITZERLAND _____

24. AUGUSTA, MAIN _____

25. VEST VIRGINIA _____

26. MOUTH DAKOTA _____

27. CARDIFF, WAILS _____

28. SANTIAGO, CHILI _____

Suggested Time: 12

Your Time: _ _ _ _ _ _ _ _ _ _ _ _

Answer on page 91

SAME ENDINGS

Each word group ends with the same three letters. Add the correct letters in the blank spaces to make words that fit the clues in the right column.

_ _ _ K E Y	Thanksgiving bird
_ _ _ K E Y	Ape
_ _ _ K E Y	Sport played with a puck
_ _ _ K E Y	Disney's Mouse
_ _ _ A C E	Castle
_ _ _ A C E	"Dennis the ___"
_ _ _ _ A C E	Small balcony
_ _ _ _ A C E	Heating device
_ _ _ _ H E R	Climate
_ _ _ H E R	Female parent
_ _ _ _ H E R	Jacket material
_ _ _ _ H E R	A sibling
_ _ _ L O W	Man
_ _ _ L O W	Go after
_ _ _ L O W	The color of butter
_ _ _ L O W	Sleep on it
_ _ _ I T S	Goes to see someone
_ _ _ I T S	Upchucks
_ _ _ I T S	Peaches, pears, plums, etc.
_ _ _ _ I T S	Hares

48

_ _ _ E N D	Pal
_ _ _ E N D	Story that's passed down through generations
_ _ _ _ _ E N D	Saturday and Sunday
_ _ _ _ _ E N D	Go from a higher to a lower place
_ _ _ _ _ _ A T E	Make prettier
_ _ _ _ A T E	Give to charity
_ _ _ _ A T E	Sea robber
_ _ _ _ A T E	Find
_ _ _ I C E	City in Italy
_ _ _ I C E	Workplace
_ _ I C E	She visited Wonderland
_ _ _ I C E	Cops
_ _ _ I N K	Get smaller
_ _ I N K	Open and close your eyes quickly
_ _ I N K	Smell
_ _ I N K	Have an opinion
_ _ A C T	Precise
_ _ _ _ _ _ A C T	Take away, in math
_ _ _ _ _ A C T	Type of lens
_ _ _ _ _ _ A C T	Legal agreement

Suggested Time: 10
Your Time: _____

Answer on page 92

DOUBLE CROSS

In the list below there are 9 types of TREES and 7 types of GEMSTONES. Each word will fit into **one** place in **one** of the grids on the opposite page. Start with the letters that have been filled in already and place each word into its correct spot. Cross off each word after you write it in the grid.

3 Letters

OAK

YEW

4 Letters

ONYX

RUBY

5 Letters

CEDAR

CORAL

EBONY

HAZEL

TOPAZ

6 Letters

CHERRY

LOCUST

WALNUT

ZIRCON

8 Letters

AMETHYST

CHESTNUT

SAPPHIRE

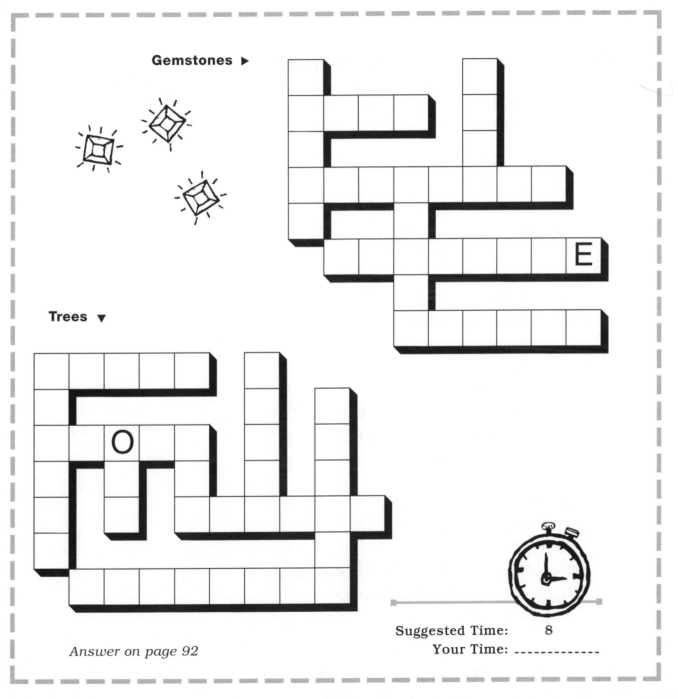

Gemstones ▶

Trees ▼

E

O

Answer on page 92

Suggested Time: 8
Your Time: _____

51

Movies you've never seen

The movie "titles" on this page are weaker versions of the real movies on the opposite page. Can you match up the two sets? Place the letters of the real movies in the correct blank spaces on this page.

1. WATER PASSENGER   _____
2. BUY TWELVE AND SAVE   _____
3. CHALLENGE, CHALLENGE   _____
4. CHILDREN IN DUMPSTERS   _____
5. DON'T STOP CHATTERING   _____
6. FOWL RACE   _____
7. GALE IN THE TREES   _____
8. HOUSETOP MUSICIAN   _____
9. INFANT EINSTEINS   _____
10. JITTERS   _____
11. LAZY PHYSICIAN   _____
12. NEIGHBORHOOD STRANGERS   _____
13. NIGHT VISIONS IN THE WEST   _____
14. OGRES IN BUSINESS   _____
15. PLAYTHING TALE   _____
16. POWERFUL QUACKERS   _____
17. ROYALTY IN THE JUNGLE   _____
18. SHORE JOURNALS   _____
19. STRANGE TIME BEFORE THE WEEKEND   _____
20. THE PRINCE'S FATHER IS BACK   _____
21. YO COWBOY!   _____

A. *ALIENS NEXT DOOR*

B. *BABY GENIUSES*

C. *BEACH DIARIES*

D. *CALIFORNIA DREAMS*

E. *CHEAPER BY THE DOZEN*

F. *CHICKEN RUN*

G. *DOCTOR DOLITTLE*

H. *DOUBLE DARE*

I. *FIDDLER ON THE ROOF*

J. *FREAKY FRIDAY*

K. *GARBAGE PAIL KIDS*

L. *GOOSEBUMPS*

M. *HEY DUDE*

N. *KEEP TALKING*

O. *MIGHTY DUCKS*

P. *MONSTERS, INC.*

Q. *RETURN OF THE KING*

R. *THE LION KING*

S. *THE WIND IN THE WILLOWS*

T *TOY STORY*

U. *WHALE RIDER*

Suggested Time: 7
Your Time: ------------

Answer on page 92

53

Sound System

Read the words below and think of a homophone for each one. A homophone is a word that sounds the same as the word listed below but is spelled differently and has a different meaning. There may be more than one homophone for each word. Let the number of letters in the grid be your guide. Write the homophone in the grid, making sure you match up the clue numbers. Then read down the starred column to find the three-word answer to this riddle:

Why was the plumber so tired?

1. **WEAR**
2. **MUSCLES**
3. **FLEW**
4. **DEAR**
5. **WAIL**
6. **WRAPPED**
7. **ALLOWED**
8. **BREWS**
9. **MAIZE**
10. **AISLE**
11. **NIGHT**
12. **ATE**
13. **ROAD**

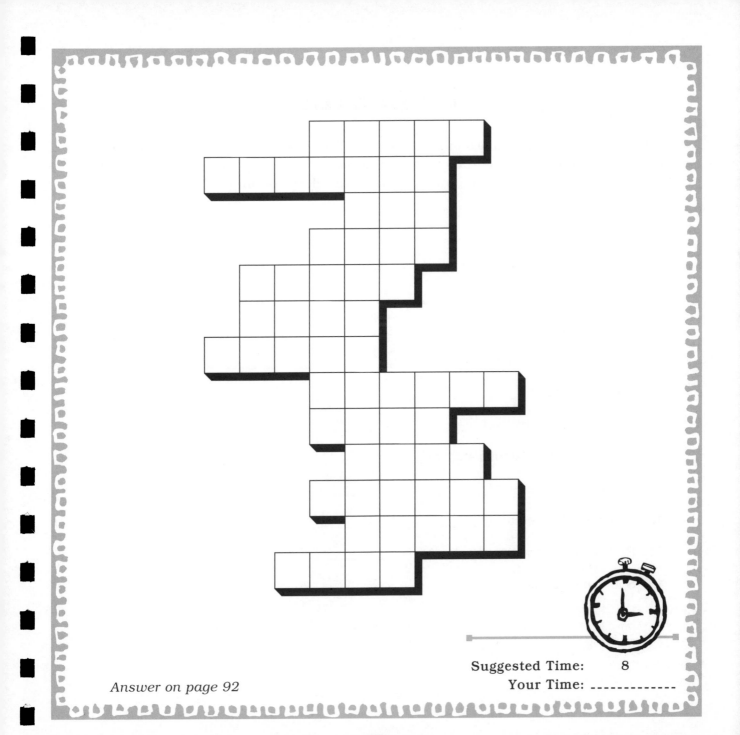

Answer on page 92

Suggested Time: 8

Your Time: -------------

55

NAME GAME

Bits and pieces of the names of some famous folks (real and fake) are in the circles on the opposite page. Use the clues on this page to identify each famous person. Write each person's full name next to his or her description. Spelling counts!

1. Bart's father _____

2. Comic actor who starred in *Daddy Day Care* _____

3. Daughter of Bill and Hillary _____

4. First American female astronaut _____

5. Queen Elizabeth's grandson _____

6. Genius physicist _____

7. She wrote *Little Women* _____

8. Hogwart's most famous student _____

9. One of the Spice Girls _____

10. Phonograph inventor _____

11. Red Cross founder _____

12. She loves Kermit _____

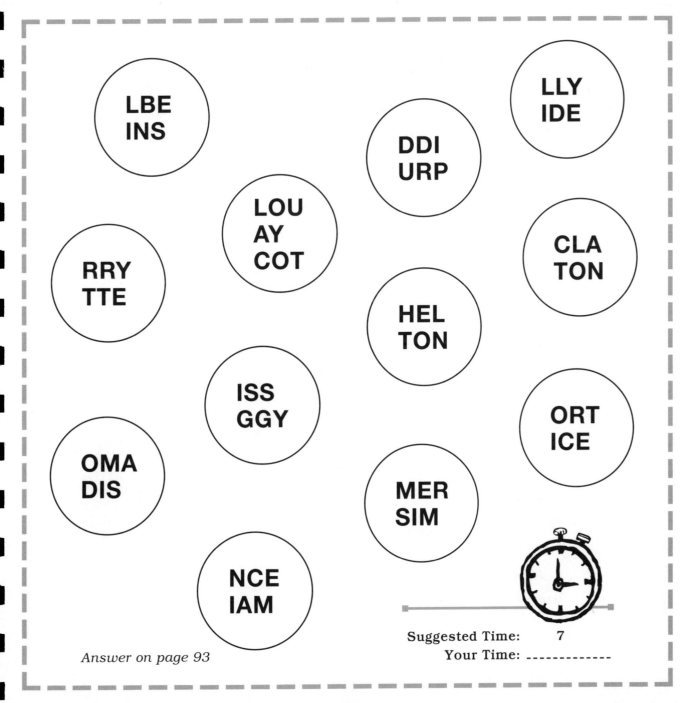

LBE INS

LLY IDE

DDI URP

LOU AY COT

CLA TON

RRY TTE

HEL TON

ISS GGY

ORT ICE

OMA DIS

MER SIM

NCE IAM

Answer on page 93

Suggested Time: 7

Your Time: -------------

57

HOUSE IT GOING?

Each word will fit into just one spot in the grid on the opposite page. Work from the letters that are already in the grid.

4 Letters

ARCH

DECK

DOOR

LOFT

POST

ROOF

ROOM

STEP

WALL

YARD

5 Letters

FLOOR

FOYER

PORCH

STUDY

6 Letters

CLOSET

COLUMN

GARRET

MANTEL

OFFICE

PANTRY

STAIRS

STUDIO

WINDOW

7 Letters

CABINET

RAILING

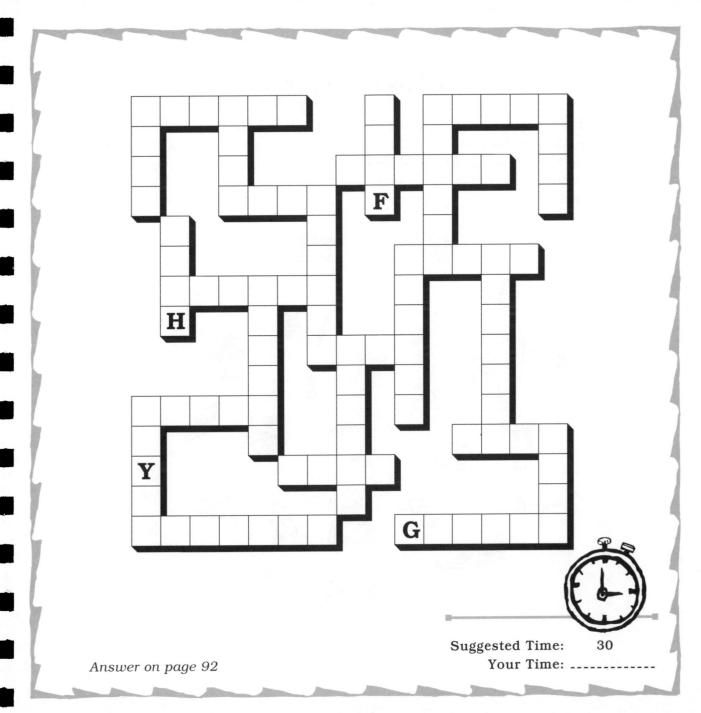

Answer on page 92

Suggested Time: 30

Your Time: _ _ _ _ _ _ _ _ _ _ _ _ _

Memory Test 3

How good is your memory? Study this group of 26 objects that begin with the 26 letters of the alphabet for up to three (3) minutes and then close the book. Then list as many items as you can on a piece of paper. You are relying solely on your memory of what you've seen. To help you with scoring, an alphabetical list appears in the answer section.

Answer on page 93

JOB SEARCH

Put one letter of the alphabet into each blank space to name a job. Cross off each letter after you use it.

A B C D E F G H I J K L M N O P Q R S T U V W X Y Z

ACTO __ __

__ ECRETARY

LAW __ ER

JANI __ OR

__ STRONOMER

E __ PLORER

PI __ OT

SAL __ SPERSON

TOUR G __ IDE

DISK __ OCKEY

E __ ITOR

BAR __ ER

RECE __ TIONIST

TA __ LOR

MA __ ICIAN

BA __ ER

S __ UASH PRO

MEC __ ANIC

__ URSE

DOCT __ R

A __ COUNTANT

__ RITER

CHE __

__ OOKEEPER

__ ETERINARIAN

__ USICIAN

Answer on page 93

Suggested Time: 4

Your Time: ------------

TWOFERS

Put the same two letters in each set of blanks to make an 8-letter word or a hyphenated word that fits the clue in the [ ].

Example: M _ _ I N _ _ A [type of pasta sauce] = M A R I N A R A

1. T _ _ R I _ _ S   [types of dogs]

2. L _ _ G U _ _ E   [flat, narrow pasta]

3. B _ _ K P _ _ K   [hiker's carrying case]

4. S _ _ V E _ _ P   [part of a kitchen appliance]

5. C _ _ F R _ _ T   [meet face-to-face]

6. T _ _ E M _ _ T   [run-down building]

7. S _ _ U R _ _ E   [soak thoroughly]

8. M _ _ S I _ _ T   [sloppiest]

9. L _ _ O R _ _ E   [chewy, stringy candy that's red or black]

10. D _ _ G U _ _ E   [masquerade]

11. C _ _ K B _ _ K   [collection of recipes]

12. F _ _ E W _ _ D   [page at the beginning of a book]

13. H _ _ S H _ _ S   [important people in an organization]

14. D _ _ N T _ _ N   [city area where businesses and shops are located]

15. C _ _ S C _ _ S   [Middle Eastern semolina dish]

16. C _ _ O - C _ _ O   [noise made by a train]

17. H _ _ H - H _ _ H   [top secret]

18. S _ _ N G _ _ I   [city in China]

19. P _ _ P A _ _ D   [ready]

20. B _ _ T L _ _ D   [number of people on a ship]

21. M _ _ S O _ _ S   [rainy seasons in Asia]

Answer on page 93

FIVE TO NINE

Fill in the fifth space on each line to form an ordinary nine-letter word. Then read down the column to answer this riddle: What musical group can open any door?

```
A D V A __ T A G E
F A T T __ N I N G
S H I P __ R E C K

C L O C __ W O R K
O B E D __ E N C E
S W O R __ F I S H
A R M I __ T I C E

C U S T __ D I A N
O R G A __ I Z E D

Q U A R __ E R L Y
W O R T __ L E S S
F L O W __ R P O T

K N O W __ E D G E
G L A M __ R O U S
M O L E __ U L E S
T W I N __ L I N G
```

Now do the same thing again to answer this riddle: What kind of doctors make fish look younger?

E Q U I _ M E N T
M I S P _ A C E D
Q U O T _ T I O N
N E C E _ S A R Y
F R A C _ U R E D
H A P P _ N E S S
D E M O _ R A C Y

V A N I _ H I N G
E X I S _ E N C E
C E N T _ R I E S
M E M O _ I Z E D
N A V I _ A T O R
O R C H _ S T R A
M Y T H _ L O G Y
B I L I _ G U A L
H O R O _ C O P E

Answer on page 94

ANNA GRAM

There are no definitions to figure out in Anna Gram's crossword. Instead, you have to rearrange the letters of each word and write them in the grid. Example: HORSE can be changed to SHORE. However, some words can be unscrambled to make more than one word, so be very careful! Make sure that the words you put into the grid work both Across and Down.

ACROSS

1. HORSE
3. CHARTS
5. DYNAMO
7. ORGANS
8. EXCEPT
11. MESA
12. SECURE
13. NEPAL
15. FIRED
19. TROUT
21. ALTER
22. TEAS

DOWN

1. WINGS
2. TUNA
3. SNEAK
4. EARTH
5. MERITS
6. MOPE
9. CLEATS
10. CARE
11. POSH
14. STARER
15. FOSTER
16. AIDE
17. HISSED
18. LAME
19. RATE
20. BORE

Answer on page 94

Suggested Time: 35

Your Time: ------------

CREWEL AND UNUSUAL PUNISHMENT

Place each word from this page into a blank space on the opposite page to form a sentence that makes sense if you're thinking punny! Reading the words ALLOWED really helps!

AISLE
AUTO
BAYOU
BOBBIN
CANOE
COUNTER
DECIDE
DRESSER
FIDDLESTICK
FISSION
JUDGEMENT
KETCHUP
MORON
NAPKIN
PRESSURE
RAISIN
RAVEN
TEAMMATE
VIOLINS
WINSOME

1. SHE OPENED HER PIGGY BANK TO _____ MONEY.

2. DO YOU KNOW ANY _____ THAT SUBJECT?

3. USE THE IRON TO _____ PANTS.

4. YOU _____ GO HOME.

5. PLEASE PAINT _____ OF THE HOUSE.

6. YOU'LL NEVER _____ TO THE FAST RUNNER.

7. GRANDMA IS ALWAYS _____ ABOUT HER GRANDCHILDREN.

8. YOU MIGHT _____ OF THE GAMES.

9. THE _____ TO RULE FAIRLY DURING THE TRIAL.

10. A SHORT _____ REFRESH YOU.

11. _____ BE BACK IN A FEW MINUTES.

12. THE FAMILY WENT ON A _____ TRIP.

13. _____ GO TO THE STORE FOR ME?

14. THE WHOLE _____ LUNCH TOGETHER.

15. THEY WANT TO CATCH SOME _____ THE SUN.

16. BUCKLE _____ TO HIS CAR SEAT.

17. THERE IS TOO MUCH _____ ON TV.

18. THE LITTLE GIRL CAN _____ SELF.

19. THE NEW STUDENT WANTS TO SIT _____.

20. IF YOUR PANTS ARE TOO SHORT YOUR _____ OUT.

Answer on page 95

Suggested Time: 15

Your Time: _____

SIX TO ELEVEN

Fill in the sixth space on each line to form an ordinary eleven-letter word. Then read down the column to finish this riddle: Why wouldn't the teacher let a student bring its chicken to school? Because the teacher didn't want to . . .

```
W  O  O  D  C  _  O  P  P  E  R
A  N  N  I  V  _  R  S  A  R  Y
P  R  O  G  R  _  M  M  I  N  G
G  I  N  G  E  _  B  R  E  A  D

C  E  R  T  I  _  I  C  A  T  E
M  I  L  L  I  _  N  A  I  R  E
U  N  D  E  R  _  E  I  G  H  T
R  E  P  U  B  _  I  C  A  N  S

T  R  A  N  S  _  A  T  I  O  N
H  Y  P  E  R  _  C  T  I  V  E
A  P  P  O  I  _  T  M  E  N  T
U  N  D  E  R  _  R  O  U  N  D
I  N  S  T  R  _  C  T  I  O  N
S  C  H  O  L  _  R  S  H  I  P
P  H  O  T  O  _  R  A  P  H  Y
F  U  R  T  H  _  R  M  O  R  E
```

Now do the same thing again to finish this riddle: Why did the bean help an old person across the street? He wanted to . . .

```
M  A  L  A  D  __  U  S  T  E  D
D  O  W  N  L  __  A  D  I  N  G
B  A  B  Y  S  __  T  T  I  N  G
F  O  R  T  U  __  A  T  E  L  Y

S  Y  M  P  A  __  H  E  T  I  C
P  R  E  S  C  __  O  O  L  E  R
B  O  O  K  K  __  E  P  I  N  G

W  H  E  E  L  __  A  R  R  O  W
S  P  E  E  D  __  M  E  T  E  R
A  E  R  O  D  __  N  A  M  I  C

M  I  C  R  O  __  C  O  P  I  C
A  T  M  O  S  __  H  E  R  E  S
I  N  T  E  R  __  U  P  T  E  D
E  N  V  I  R  __  N  M  E  N  T
P  A  S  T  E  __  R  I  Z  E  D
T  E  R  R  I  __  O  R  I  E  S
S  I  G  H  T  __  E  E  I  N  G
```

Suggested Time: 5
Your Time: -------------

Answer on page 94

NUMBER CROSSWORD

Fill in the blanks with numbers instead of letters. Some clues are just simple arithmetic problems, while others are related to each other. Start with all the arithmetic problems and work from there. You can use a calculator or even your fingers and toes!

ACROSS

1. 5 plus 6
3. 1 Across plus 14
5. 3 Across times 20
6. 5 Across plus 5
8. 1 Across doubled
9. 3 Across plus 49
10. One-half of 9 Across
12. 1000 plus 115
15. 6 Across minus 23
16. 1 Across times 7
17. 16 Across plus 4
18. 1 less than 5 Across
20. 12 Across times 3
22. 2 less than 10 Across
23. 22 Across doubled
24. 23 Across minus 18
26. 300 plus 225
28. 226 plus 200
29. 30 plus 60
30. 29 Across plus 8

DOWN

1. 700 plus 321
2. 1 less than 1 Across
3. Half of 508
4. 3 Across doubled
5. 2 more than 4 Down
7. 300 plus 238
9. 4 Down plus 3 Across
11. 9 Across minus 2
13. 100 plus 79
14. 2 Down plus 7
15. 207 doubled
17. 57 plus 26
18. 4 Down minus 7
19. 191 times 5
20. 2 Down times 3
21. 2764 plus 2764
23. 9 Down times 10
25. 1 more than 3 Across
27. 3 more than 25 Down
28. 1 Less than 4 Down

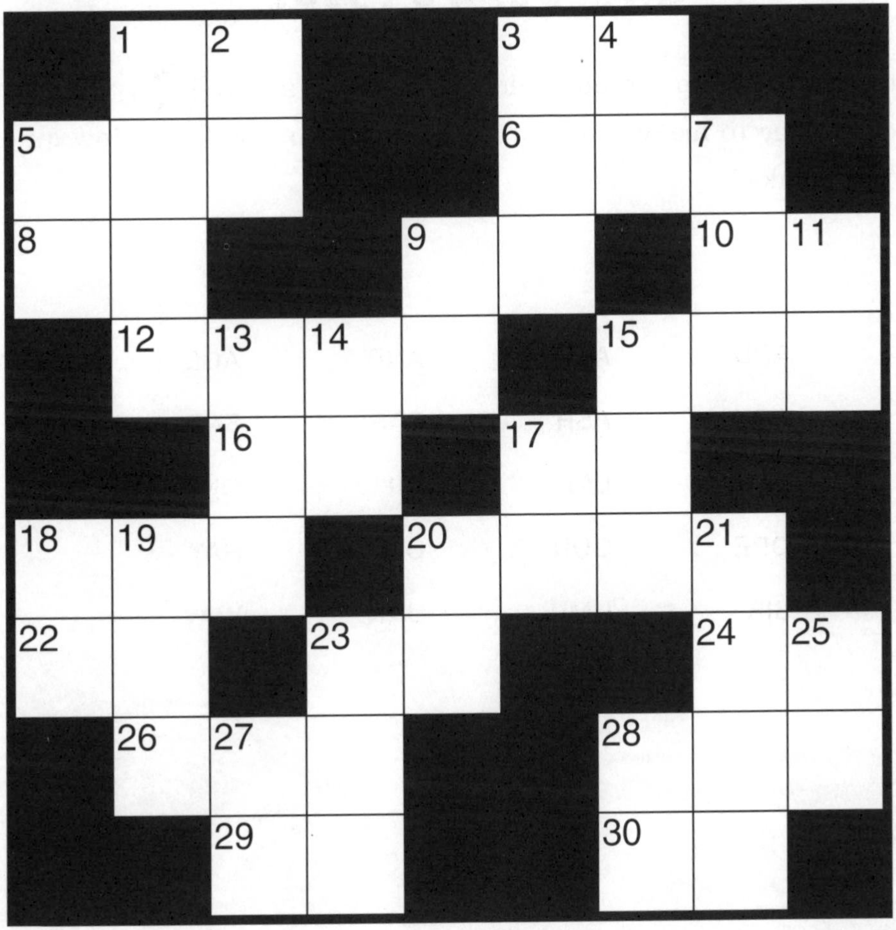

Suggested Time: 45

Your Time: ____________

Answer on page 95

INSIDE/OUTSIDE

One three-letter word from the box below will fit into a four-letter word in the list on the opposite page to make a new word described in the [ ]. How quickly can you fill up the blanks?

ADD	ALL	AND	AGE
ARK	ASH	EAR	END
LAX	LAY	OIL	ONE
ORE	OUR	OUT	RAY
SIR	UMP	URN	WAY

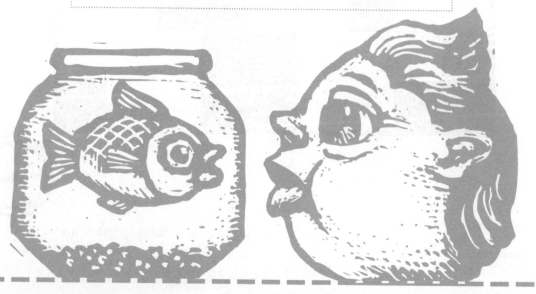

1. D E __ __ __ E D   [Longed for]

2. W __ __ __ I N G   [Doing laundry]

3. S __ __ __ I N G   [Moving back and forth to music]

4. S H __ __ __ O W   [Like a wading pool]

5. P O __ __ __ S T   [Having the least money]

6. S P __ __ __ E D   [Ruined]

7. S H __ __ __ E D   [Screamed]

8. N __ __ __ E S T   [Closest]

9. F __ __ __ I S H   [Supply with tables, chairs, etc.]

10. D E __ __ __ E D   [Postponed]

11. C __ __ __ O N S   [Drawing items}

12. G R __ __ __ A D   [Close relative}

13. P __ __ __ A N T   [Ornament on a necklace]

14. C __ __ __ __ A G E   [Bravery]

15. P __ __ __ A N T   [Elaborate spectacle]

16. P __ __ __ I E S   [Rice fields]

17. R E __ __ __ E D   [Took a break]

18. P I __ __ __ E R   [First person to settle in a territory]

19. S L __ __ __ E D   [Slouched down]

20. P __ __ __ I N G   [Putting a car into a garage]

Suggested Time: 10

Your Time: -------------

Answer on page 95

PRESS RELEASE

A new cultural club sent the following press release to the local newspaper and asked if it could be printed in the next edition. However, before the entertainment editor could print the release, she had to change the 33 mistakes written in **boldfaced** type. Some words had been changed to anagrams while others had been made into homophones. Write the correct words on the blanks on the opposite page.

The **THORN HORSE RATS** League will **HOLED TIS** annual fund-**RAZING** event on **DYNAMO THING**. The event is a combination gourmet dinner and art **HOWS**. A **FOR**-course **LAME** will **BEE VERSED**. **ALTER**, **AWL** guests **ERA** invited to enter **THEE** museum **TWO** view the works on display.

Dinner will consist of:

> Mixed **ABBY** salad greens
>
> Split **APE OPUS**
>
> T-bone **STAKE** with **SHAMED** potatoes and corn
>
> Chocolate **MOOSE**
>
> Coffee, **ATE**, cocoa, and milk will also be available.

STRAITS represented **HEAR** are local painters and sculptors **HOW** created works specifically **FOUR** the event. All **MITES** can be purchased **HEWN** the show is over. Contact the League **WON** to **BYE** your tickets to this gala event.

1. _____
2. _____
3. _____
4. _____
5. _____
6. _____
7. _____
8. _____
9. _____
10. _____
11. _____
12. _____
13. _____
14. _____
15. _____
16. _____
17. _____
18. _____
19. _____

20. _____
21. _____
22. _____
23. _____
24. _____
25. _____
26. _____
27. _____
28. _____
29. _____
30. _____
31. _____
32. _____
33. _____

Answer on page 95

Suggested Time: 10
Your Time: ------------

SHORT AND SWEET

Why use long sentences when a one-word answer will do? Place these 29 words into the grid on the opposite page. Start with the letters already in the grid and work from there.

2 Letters
NO
OH
UM

3 Letters
GEE
HOW?
MAN
NOW
WHY?
YEP

4 Letters
AHOY
GOSH
LET'S
NEXT
PHEW
STOP
TIME

5 Letters
HELLO
LATER
MAYBE
PSHAW
READY
YIPES

6 Letters
ENOUGH
INDEED
REALLY
SURELY
YOO-HOO

7 Letters
GANGWAY
IMAGINE

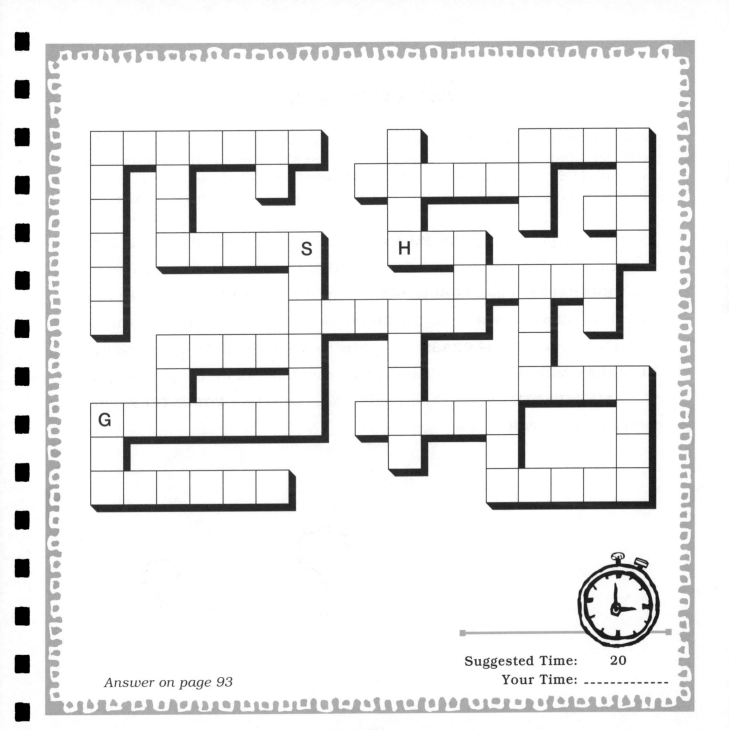

Answer on page 93

Suggested Time: 20

Your Time: ------------

79

Mystery bio

Read this profile of a famous person. To discover his or her name, put only the boldfaced words from the story into the grid. Use the letters that are already in the grid PLUS the number of letters in each word (or phrase) as a guide. When the grid is complete, read down one of the columns to find this person's identity.

I was born in 1819 in **LONG ISLAND**, New York, where I was the third of eight children. When I was in my 20s and 30s I worked in **JOURNALISM** as the editor of a **NEWSPAPER**. I also **PUBLISHED** a book of my **POEMS** in 1855. The first edition had 12 poems, but by the **THIRD** edition there were 130 poems. The name of this book was Leaves of **GRASS**. My poetry book was one of the most important **LITERARY** books in American history. I am sometimes called the greatest poet of the **NINETEENTH** century. During my lifetime I was also a **VOLUNTEER** nurse during the Civil **WAR**.

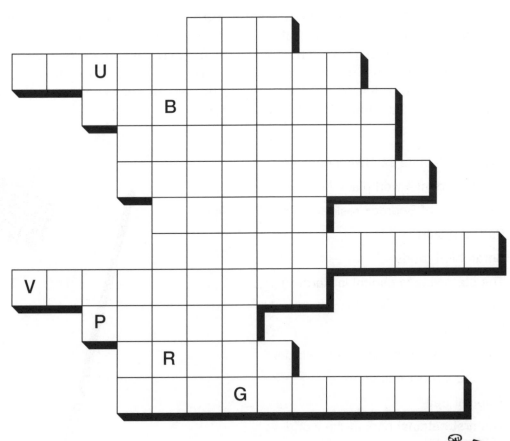

Answer on page 96

Suggested Time: 15
Your Time: -------------

81

CLEAR OUT

Find the answer to each clue in the same numbered row in the diagram on the opposite page. Cross off the clue, letter by letter. All the letters of an answer will be next to each other, but there will always be an extra letter or two on each line. When you've cleared out the grid, put the LEFTOVER letters into the spaces below the diagram. Go from left to right and top to bottom to answer this riddle: Why did King Kong wear a baseball glove to the airport?

1. Purple flower

1. Black-and-white sandwich cookies

2. The President's workplace (two words)

3. Last name of Bedrock residents Fred and Wilma

4. Part of a shirt

4. Scrambled foods

5. The state whose capital is Hartford

6. Animal from Peru with long woolly hair

6. Bedspread

7. Star of The Rolling Stones (2 words)

8. Second largest continent

8. Tropical fruit

9. The first national park in the world

10. Mexican food

10. 13th American President ___ Fillmore

11. Teeth used for grinding food

11. Capital of Norway

12. Nursery rhyme character (3 words)

1	H	L	I	L	A	C	E	O	R	E	O	S
2	O	V	A	L	O	F	F	I	C	E	H	A
3	D	T	F	L	I	N	T	S	T	O	N	E
4	C	O	L	L	A	R	O	E	G	G	S	C
5	A	C	O	N	N	E	C	T	I	C	U	T
6	A	L	P	A	C	A	T	Q	U	I	L	T
7	C	H	M	I	C	K	J	A	G	G	E	R
8	A	F	R	I	C	A	A	G	U	A	V	A
9	P	Y	E	L	L	O	W	S	T	O	N	E
10	T	A	C	O	L	M	I	L	L	A	R	D
11	M	O	L	A	R	S	A	O	S	L	O	N
12	E	O	L	D	K	I	N	G	C	O	L	E

Riddle Answer: __ __   __ __ __ __   __ __   __ __ __ __ __ __

__   __ __ __ __ __ __.

THAW WHAT?

Each sentence has two four-letter words that are anagrams of each other, like **THAW** and **WHAT**. Find and underline these words.

1. MY AUNT ORDERED TUNA FISH.
2. ERIC LOVES RICE PUDDING.
3. LUCY WILL WALK A MILE FOR A LIME DRINK.
4. THE AIDE HAD A BRIGHT IDEA.
5. SHE BOUGHT AN ICE-CREAM CONE ONCE.
6. RUTH GOT HURT WHEN SHE TRIPPED.
7. TAKE THE TRAM TO THE SHOPPING MART.
8. THIS IS PART OF THE TRAP DOOR.
9. THE DEAN OWNED A GREAT DANE.
10. HE SENT THE MAIL TO LIMA, PERU.
11. SAVE THE BLUE VASE FOR PETER.
12. RAMS DON'T HAVE ANY ARMS.
13. MARY JOINED THE ARMY.
14. PUT THE LAMP NEAR THE PALM TREE.
15. THE HOST SHOT SEVERAL PICTURES.
16. THERE ARE LOTS OF LOST TOYS IN THAT BOX.
17. WHO WILL EDIT THE DIET BOOK?
18. WHERE DID YOU BURY THE RUBY BRACELET?
19. THEY SOLD TIES ON THEIR WEB SITE.
20. SHE MADE STEW IN WEST VIRGINIA.

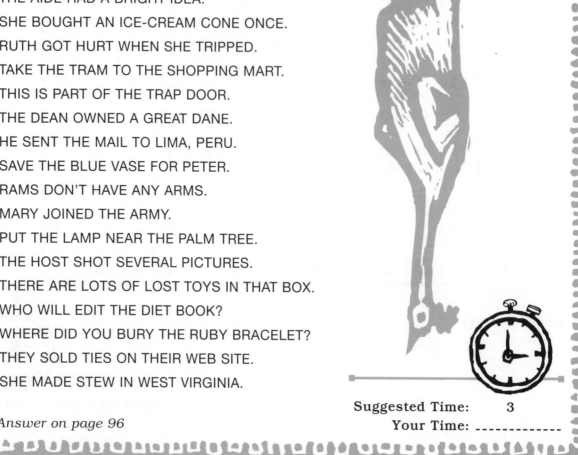

Answer on page 96

Suggested Time:　3
Your Time: ------------

84

Something's Fishy

Form the name of a fish on each line by taking a three-letter word from the box and writing it on the blank spaces.

ARK	BAR	BUT	CAR
CAT	DIN	HAD	HER
HIT	MAC	NAP	NOW
OLD	OUT	PER	RAN

1. H A L I __ __ __
2. G __ __ __ F I S H
3. __ __ __ R A C U D A
4. T R __ __ __ __
5. __ __ __ R I N G
6. M I N __ __ __
7. P I __ __ __ H A
8. __ __ __ F I S H

9. __ __ __ D O C K
10. __ __ __ P
11. __ __ __ C H
12. S A R __ __ __ E
13. S __ __ __ P E R
14. __ __ __ K E R E L
15. S H __ __ __
16. W __ __ __ E F I S H

Suggested Time: 4

Your Time: ------------

Answer on page 96

CITY CENTER

All the letters in both words on each line are the same EXCEPT for one extra letter. Write the extra letter in the blank space and then read DOWN to find the name of a capital city.

AMHERST ___ HEARTS

RESTON ___ STERN

BOSTON ___ BOOTS

BUTTE ___ TUBE

PATERSON ___ SENATOR

DARIEN ___ DRAIN

SALEM ___ SEAM

HIRAM ___ HARM

ODESSA ___ SODAS

NEWARK ___ WAKEN

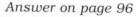

Suggested Time: 2
Your Time: _____

Answer on page 96

FOOD FUN

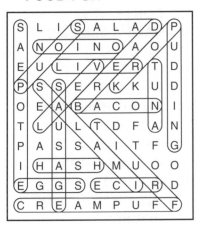

Answer: . . . liked fast food.

ALPHA-RIDDLE

```
A B D O M E N
  A C C O R D
  A C C O U N T
  A D D I N G
  A D E P T
    A D O R A B L E
    A F R A I D
A G H A S T
      A H O Y
      A I M L E S S
    A L L O W A N C E
    A M E R I C A N
    A N G E R E D
```

Answer:
Mount Rashmore

MYSTERY NUMBER

A. 14
B. 34
C. 36
D. 54
E. 18
F. 75
G. 67
H. 63
I. 17
J. 15
K. 79
L. 42

Mystery number = 43

MEMORY TEST 1

5 out of 10 = Good
7 or above = Great!

1. Umbrella
2. Mainville
3. Three
4. None
5. Eight
6. Four
7. $2.50
8. 5:00
9. The vendor's shirt doesn't have horizontal or vertical stripes.
10. Dress

END/START

1. Mascot/Cottage
2. Parrot/Rotunda
3. Bobcat/Catalog
4. Combat/Bathtub
5. Tactic/Tickled
6. Muffin/Finally
7. Ocelot/Lottery
8. Carpet/Petunia
9. Rubbed/Bedroom
10. Format/Matador
11. Mutant/Antonym
12. Sorrow/Rowboat
13. Recall/Allergy
14. Appear/Earache
15. Unless/Essence

ANSWERING SERVICE

Odd
Face
Sick
Ran

Answer: In a deck of cards

Love
Mad
Park
Tie

Answer: Evaporated milk

NOT SO SYMBOL

The identical squares are:
2, 3, 8, 10, 14, 18

HAPPY/SAD

Giggle
Howl
Crack up
Chuckle
Smile
Grin
Roar
Burst a gut
Sob
Weep
Wail
Break down
Blubber
Bawl
Whimper
Shriek

ON THE ROAD

Answer: Gridlock

HIDDEN NAMES

1. BAG A RYE BREAD FOR THE CUSTOMER.
2. CAN YOU READ A LETTER?
3. DON'T SEND CASH TO NEW FRIENDS.
4. FINISH THIS AND YOU CAN LEAVE.
5. GET HELP IF YOU NEED IT.
6. I FED THE GERBIL LAST TIME.
7. IS THAT LEAD OR IS IT GOLD?
8. IT'S HER EAR THAT HURTS.
9. LET HANDYMEN DO THE WORK.
10. LOOK AT THEM MAMA!
11. SHE CAN'T SELL ENOUGH CLOTHING.
12. SHE LOST A NEW COAT.
13. SHE'S LEARNING RIDICULOUS JOKES.
14. THAT COMPANY WILL MERGE OR GET SOLD.
15. THE COOK FRIED APPLES.
16. THE WOMAN DREW PORTRAITS.
17. WALK A MILE ON SUNDAY.
18. WE WENT OUT LAST EVENING.
19. WHICH RISK WILL HE TAKE?
20. YOU SHOULD VISIT FRANCE SOON.
21. IS THE BARN OLDER THAN THE HOUSE?
22. DON'T MAR YOUR COUNTER TOP.
23. I HAD A MEAL AT THE DINER.
24. THE MARLIN DARTED ABOUT.
25. THE ODOR EMANATED FROM THE KITCHEN.
26. THREE RAJAS ONLY WANTED TO SING.
27. DO UGLY PETS GET PAMPERED?
28. IS YOUR CAR OLDER THAN MINE?
29. I AM ON A DIET.
30. HAVE YOU HAD A PEAR LATELY?

MAKEOVERS

1. i
2. j
3. b
4. o
5. c
6. e
7. p
8. l
9. r
10. f
11. q
12. n
13. d
14. h
15. g
16. s
17. a
18. m
19. v
20. k
21. u
22. t

THE WRITE STUFF

1. DANGEROUS STREET CROSSINGS by Jay Walker
2. CARD GAMES by Ace S. Wilde
3. DINING OUT ALL THE TIME by Kent Cook
4. THE DESSERT COOKBOOK by B. Sweet
5. SYNTHETIC FABRICS by Polly Ester
6. GAMES FOR TODDLERS by Hy Dan Seek
7. ROUND ABOUT by Sir Cull
8. HOW TO MAKE MILLIONS by Rich Mann
9. CREATIVE JEWELRY by Sterling Silver
10. YEWS, PINES, AND CEDARS by Forest Ranger
11. CALL ME ROMEO by Hart Braker
12. MIRACLE MEDICINE by Ann T. Biotic
13. THE BIG CHEESE by Val V. Ta
14. THE MOVING MANUAL by Van Driver

STATE DEPARTMENT

I	N	G	S	T	S	T	P	H	P	M	I	V
N	O	R	T	H	C	A	R	O	L	I	N	A
C	R	E	R	R	O	U	A	N	A	N	V	N
O	M	A	E	E	R	G	G	E	N	U	I	I
M	A	S	S	A	C	H	U	S	E	T	T	S
E	L	Y	S	D	H	T	E	T	T	E	E	H

Answer: North Carolina and Massachusetts

JUST THE OPPOSITE

1. Win — Lose
2. Sharp — Blunt
3. Smile — Frown
4. Real — Fake
5. Nice — Mean
6. Hot — Cold
7. Fast — Slow
8. Give — Take
9. Tame — Wild
10. Whole — Part
11. Polite — Rude
12. Up — Down
13. Fall — Spring
14. Love — Hate
15. Mine — Yours
16. Tall — Short
17. Wide — Narrow
18. Sick — Well
19. Fat — Thin
20. Rich — Poor
21. Low — High
22. Open — Close
23. Good — Bad
24. War — Peace
25. Sweet — Sour
26. Right — Wrong

Answers

"P" IS FOR PUZZLE

CARRYING CASES

VACATION PLACES

TUNED IN

1. Best test
2. Small hall
3. Far car
4. Weak beak
5. Fake cake
6. Real meal
7. Big wig
8. Nice ice
9. Jelly belly
10. Night sight
11. Mum bum
12. Whole pole
13. Jail wail
14. Pink sink
15. June spoon
16. Lime dime
17. Get jet
18. Nest guest
19. Cool pool
20. New glue
21. Plain chain
22. Pail scale
23. Fox box
24. Fling ring

MEMORY TEST 2

12–17 out of 25 = Good
18 or above = Great!

1. cake
2. camel
3. camera
4. candle
5. candy cane
6. canoe
7. car
8. carrot
9. cat
10. caterpillar
11. chair
12. cheese
13. chicken
14. cigarette
15. clock
16. clothes pin
17. comb
18. computer
19. cone (ice cream)
20. corn
21. cow
22. crayon
23. crab
24. cup
25. cupcake

FIRST LADIES

Answer: Jacqueline
Kennedy

SQUEEZE PLAY

1. Cambodia and Jordan
2. Diapers and Bottles
3. Chrysler and Cadillac
4. November and Tuesday
5. Cougar and Chipmunk
6. Lobster and Clams
7. Kelly and Moss
8. Nectar and Punch
9. Yogurt and Cream
10. Harvard and Princeton
11. Croquet and Badminton
12. Scorpio and Gemini
13. Pinkie and Thumb
14. Limbo and Waltz
15. Omelet and Pancake
16. Hungarian and Swedish
17. Sophomore and Junior
18. Zipper and Button
19. Volvo and Saab
20. Mayor and President
21. Mariners and Yankees
22. Karate and Judo
23. Geometry and Algebra
24. Zucchini and Eggplant

CUT IT OUT

A <u>li</u>ttle boy ru<u>shed</u> by a <u>police</u> <u>off</u>icer. Five m<u>in</u>utes <u>later</u> he <u>dashed</u> by ag<u>ain</u>. After <u>doing</u> <u>th</u>is s<u>ever</u>al times <u>the</u> cop s<u>topped</u> the boy <u>and</u> <u>asked</u>, "<u>W</u>here are you <u>going</u>?"

The kid rep<u>lied</u>, "I'm <u>running</u> a<u>way</u> <u>from</u> ho<u>me</u>."

"<u>Well,</u> why are you <u>jogging</u> <u>around</u> the b<u>lock</u> so <u>many</u> <u>time</u>s?" <u>a</u>sked the cop.

The kid answe<u>red</u>, "Be<u>cause</u> my <u>mother</u> <u>won't</u> let me c<u>ross</u> the ro<u>ad</u> by my<u>self</u>."

ANIMAL ANTICS

Answer: . . . a lamb shade.

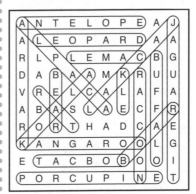

ADVENTURE TRAVEL

1. Singapore
2. New Hampshire
3. Paris, France
4. Rome, Italy
5. Seattle, Washington
6. San Jose, California
7. Great Lakes
8. Baton Rouge, Louisiana
9. Kuala Lumpur, Malaysia
10. Annapolis, Maryland
11. Amazon River
12. Rio Grande
13. Palo Alto, California
14. Austin, Texas
15. Kodiak, Alaska
16. Ann Arbor, Michigan
17. Fort Lee, New Jersey
18. Costa Rica
19. Erie, Pennsylvania
20. Reading, Pennsylvania
21. Seoul, Korea
22. Washington, D.C.
23. Bern, Switzerland
24. Augusta, Maine
25. West Virginia
26. South Dakota
27. Cardiff, Wales
28. Santiago, Chile

SAME ENDINGS

Turkey	Friend
Monkey	Legend
Hockey	Weekend
Mickey	Descend
Palace	Decorate
Menace	Donate
Terrace	Pirate
Furnace	Locate
Weather	Venice
Mother	Office
Leather	Alice
Brother	Police
Fellow	Shrink
Follow	Blink
Yellow	Stink
Pillow	Think
Visits	Exact
Vomits	Subtract
Fruits	Contact
Rabbits	Contract

DOUBLE CROSS

Gemstones

Trees

MOVIES YOU'VE NEVER SEEN

1. U	12. A
2. E	13. D
3. H	14. P
4. K	15. T
5. N	16. O
6. F	17. R
7. S	18. C
8. I	19. J
9. B	20. Q
10. L	21. M
11. G	

SOUND SYSTEM

Answer: He felt drained.

HOUSE IT GOING?

NAME GAME
1. Homer Simpson
2. Eddie Murphy
3. Chelsea Clinton
4. Sally Ride
5. Prince William
6. Albert Einstein
7. Louisa May Alcott
8. Harry Potter
9. Sporty Spice
10. Thomas Edison
11. Clara Barton
12. Miss Piggy

MEMORY TEST 3
13–18 out of 26 = Good
19 or above = Great!

1. ambulance
2. beaver
3. computer
4. drill
5. elephant
6. fox
7. ghost
8. hammer
9. iron
10. jack-o'-lantern
11. key
12. lock
13. microwave
14. nest
15. octopus
16. piano
17. queen
18. raccoon
19. shoe
20. tree
21. umbrella
22. vacuum cleaner
23. whale
24. xylophone
25. yarn
26. zipper

JOB SEARCH
Acto**r**	T**ai**lor
Secretary	Ma**g**ician
Law**y**er	Ba**k**er
Jani**t**or	**Sq**uash Pro
Astronomer	Mec**h**anic
E**x**plorer	**N**urse
Pil**o**t	Doc**t**or
Sal**e**sperson	A**c**countant
Tour G**u**ide	**W**riter
Disk **J**ockey	Che**f**
E**d**itor	**Z**ookeeper
Bar**b**er	**V**eterinarian
Rece**p**tionist	**M**usician

TWOFERS
1. Terriers
2. Linguine
3. Backpack
4. Stovetop
5. Confront
6. Tenement
7. Saturate
8. Messiest
9. Licorice
10. Disguise
11. Cookbook
12. Foreword
13. Hotshots
14. Downtown
15. Couscous
16. Choo-choo
17. Hush-hush
18. Shanghai
19. Prepared
20. Boatload
21. Monsoons

SHORT AND SWEET

FIVE TO NINE

Advantage
Fattening
Shipwreck

Clockwork
Obedience
Swordfish
Armistice

Custodian
Organized

Quarterly
Worthless
Flowerpot

Knowledge
Glamorous
Molecules
Twinkling

Answer: New Kids on the Lock

Equipment
Misplaced
Quotation
Necessary
Fractured
Happiness
Democracy

Vanishing
Existence
Centuries
Memorized
Navigator
Orchestra
Mythology
Bilingual
Horoscope

Answer: Plastic sturgeons

ANNA GRAM

SIX TO ELEVEN

Woodchopper
Anniversary
Programming
Gingerbread

Certificate
Millionaire
Underweight
Republicans

Translation
Hyperactive
Appointment
Underground
Instruction
Scholarship
Photography
Furthermore

Answer: . . . hear fowl language

Maladjusted
Downloading
Babysitting
Fortunately

Sympathetic
Preschooler
Bookkeeping

Wheelbarrow
Speedometer
Aerodynamic

M **i** c **r** o **s** c o p **i** c
A t m o **s** p **h** e r e s
I n t e **r** **r** u p t e d
E n v i r **o** n m e n t
P a s t e **u** r i z e d
T e r r i t **o** r i e s
S i g h t **s** e e i n g

Answer: . . . join the Boy Sprouts.

CREWEL AND UNUSUAL PUNISHMENT

1. Counter
2. Moron
3. Pressure
4. Auto
5. Decide
6. Ketchup
7. Raven
8. Winsome
9. Judgement
10. Napkin
11. Aisle
12. Fission
13. Canoe
14. Teammate
15. Raisin
16. Bobbin
17. Violins
18. Dresser

19. Bayou
20. Fiddlestick

NUMBER CROSSWORD

INSIDE/OUTSIDE

1. De**sired**
2. W**ashing**
3. S**waying**
4. Sh**allow**
5. Po**orest**
6. Sp**oiled**
7. Sh**outed**
8. N**earest**
9. F**urnish**
10. Del**ayed**
11. Cr**ayons**
12. Gr**andad**
13. P**endant**
14. C**ourage**
15. P**ageant**
16. P**addies**

17. Re**laxed**
18. Pi**oneer**
19. Sl**umped**
20. P**arking**

PRESS RELEASE

1. North
2. Shore
3. Arts
4. Hold
5. Its
6. Raising
7. Monday
8. Night
9. Show
10. Four
11. Meal
12. Be
13. Served
14. Later
15. All
16. Are
17. The
18. To
19. Baby
20. Pea
21. Soup
22. Steak
23. Mashed
24. Mousse
25. Tea
26. Artists
27. Here

28. Who
29. For
30. Items
31. When
32. Now
33. Buy

MYSTERY BIO

Mystery person:
Walt Whitman

CLEAR OUT

1. Lilac
1. Oreos
2. Oval office
3. Flintstone
4. Collar
4. Eggs
5. Connecticut
6. Alpaca
6. Quilt
7. Mick Jagger
8. Africa
8. Guava

9. Yellowstone
10. Taco
10. Millard
11. Molars
11. Oslo
12. Old King Cole

Answer: He had to catch a plane.

THAW WHAT?

1. Aunt/tuna
2. Eric/rice
3. Mile/lime
4. Aide/idea
5. Cone/once
6. Ruth/hurt
7. Tram/mart
8. Part/trap
9. Dean/Dane
10. Mail/Lima
11. Save/vase
12. Rams/arms
13. Mary/Army
14. Lamp/palm
15. Host/shot
16. Lots/lost
17. Edit/diet
18. Bury/ruby
19. Ties/site
20. Stew/West

SOMETHING'S FISHY

1. Hali**but**
2. **Gol**dfish
3. **Barra**cuda
4. T**rou**t
5. **Herr**ing
6. Min**now**
7. Pi**ra**nha
8. **Cat**fish
9. **Ha**ddock
10. **Car**p
11. **Per**ch
12. Sar**din**e
13. S**nap**per
14. **Mack**erel
15. Sha**rk**
16. W**hit**efish

CITY CENTER

AMHERST	M	HEARTS
RESTON	O	STERN
BOSTON	N	BOOTS
BUTTE	T	TUBE
PATERSON	P	SENATOR
DARIEN	E	DRAIN
SALEM	L	SEAM
HIRAM	I	HARM
ODESSA	E	SODAS
NEWARK	R	WAKEN

Capital city: Montpelier (Vermont)